A Divine Love Letter from The Angels

*Joyous Guidance for Transforming
Your Life from the Inside Out!*

Suzanne Bennett

Beaver's Pond Press, Inc
Edina, Minnesota

To Cheryl,
Your heart always
Knows!
With Love,
Suzanne Bennett

ISBN 10: 1-59298-126-7
ISBN 13: 978-1-59298-126-7

Library of Congress Catalog Number: 2005933685

Book design and typesetting: Mori Studio, Inc.
Cover design: Mori Studio, Inc.
Cover Photo: The handmade glass heart was created by the highly talented glass artists of Glass Eye Studio, Seattle, Washington. This "Heart of Fire" is made of dichoric glass—a special marriage of reflected and transmitted light. The effect is a mystical rainbow of color, frozen forever in solid crystal yet offering a different visual delight with each new glance.

Printed in the United States of America

First Printing: October 2005

08 07 06 05   6 5 4 3 2 1

Beaver's Pond Press, Inc.
7104 Ohms Lane, Suite 216
Edina, MN 55439
(952) 829-8818
www.BeaversPondPress.com

To order, visit www.BookHouseFulfillment.com or call 1-800-901-3480. Reseller and special sales discounts available.

To my dearest mother, Virginia,

with unending gratitude for giving my heart

wings and helping to bring to life this beautiful

volume through her great love and support.

Acknowldgements

Suzanne Bennett wishes to acknowledge all the human and angelic beings on Earth and in Heaven who have so lovingly provided their amazing talents, skills, support, and encouragement to help her create and manifest this book, especially Andrew, Kathy, David, BatCat, John, Sydney, Faye, Belinda, Rich, Marta, Elisa, Jonathan, Hosanna, Josephina, Creamsicle, Jennifer, Tom, Jaana, Milton, Kellie, Judith and Rebecca. From her heart to yours, Thank You!

Preface

The book you're holding isn't the book I thought I'd write. For many months on the way to giving birth to *this* wonderful little volume, my manuscript had the working title, *The Joyful Art of Following Your Heart*.

In it, I described in great depth the spiritual perspectives, teachings, and experiences which have comprised my journey as a heart-based spiritual educator, writer, and healer who works with the Angels. It was page after page of solid, didactic verbiage, all supposedly meant to guide its future readers in living a more joyful and heart-based life.

Yet, it didn't feel right somehow. My intuitive voice was telling me that something was amiss and off-center about this personal literary endeavor. But, intellectually, it *seemed* to make sense, to be right on target with my intention of writing a book in the first place. The confusion—and the conundrum—continued for days. So how to proceed?

Ultimately I realized I was writing a book about following one's heart *straight from my head*, directly from intellect to keyboard. I suddenly saw that I was essentially closing out my heart's voice in the process. Yikes!

The poignant irony (not to mention hypocrisy) of this head-heart disconnect was gently pointed out to me by the Deva Angels who were helping me manifest this project. Their oh-so-subtle message—and one of my biggest spiritual "ah-ha's" ever—was, as you may imagine, a major turning point in this endeavor!

I had been trying to work on the book when, at my feet, my book-writing companion—my kitty, named BatCat—literally shook (well, tilted) his head, simultaneously yawning and rolling his eyes. His message was quite obvious: "Please drop the preachy ego voice and get on with sharing your heart's story." I howled with laughter. Clearly, the time had arrived for me to set aside the old manuscript. And so I did.

Bright and early the next morning, a kinder, gentler book began to take shape. It turns out my heart had a very different story to tell and a different message to share. And I discovered a softer, more compassionate way of sharing with the world the amazing and profound Angelic wisdom that has transformed my life, the lives of my clients, and the lives of all of those around me.

Guidance from the Angels has dramatically improved every facet of my life: I've been a better parent, friend, colleague, daughter, sister, neighbor, and spouse. I've felt the impact in my career as a healer and educator, in my financial life, and in my physical and emotional health and healing. I've grown in virtually **every** aspect of my being: body, mind, heart, soul, and spirit, inside and out. And these have been joyous and welcome changes, improvements that are deep, wide, and enduring. They truly have provided me with all that my heart desires.

And so, I invite you to pause for a moment and imagine just how life—**your life**—would be if it were filled with all that **your heart** desires. **Everything** your heart desires. Beginning today. Sound appealing? Then please read on. The inspiration and wisdom directly from the Angels to YOU is here to help you create this life. The joyful opportunity to receive this help is yours.

Blessings for a joyful, enchanting,

and enlightened journey!

My Heart's Story

For many years early in my life, I so wished to receive a letter like the one in this book. Like so many of us, I sometimes try to imagine what my life might have been like if, as a child or young adult, I'd been told that I was perfect and was loved unconditionally in a way I could really hear and understand. What if I had been told that I was worthy of receiving all that my heart desired, not by virtue of what I did for other folks, or earned, or accomplished in the outer world, but because of who I was, a beloved Child of God? What if I had learned as a child that expressing the truth and the creative voice of my heart was an important, sacred, and necessary endeavor, that Angelic assistance in all matters was available to me just for the asking?

For me, that letter actually did "arrive" from the Angels, but not until I was in my mid-40s and beginning to reawaken spiritually, to embrace fully my soul's journey and my heart's leadership in fulfilling my life's purpose. But I'm getting ahead of myself. The story really begins nearly half a century ago.

I often speak of my life journey as the "Path of Plush Wisdom." You see, I have always loved plush critters, or stuffed animals, which the Angels have taught me are inanimate pets. Actually, to be precise, they are Nature Angels and are in our lives to help us heal emotionally. As a young girl, I surrounded myself with a happy abundance of them. I regularly assembled my beloved plush friends for delightful, spontaneous backyard or fireside tea parties. Each venue—

the glowing hearth and that emerald expanse of lawn—was a source of much comfort and joy. Each was, for me, a magical oasis of contentment, my very own piece of Heaven on Earth. Time spent in either place was a welcome escape, especially when, as an older child, I had to deal with the sadness and challenges of living in the emotionally stifling reality of an alcoholic home and repressive school.

But, when I was still young, I engaged in life with a completely open and trusting heart. Creative expression of all sorts came naturally to me, especially on stage as an actress. I freely and fearlessly embraced it, joyfully participating in the local children's theatre, in school plays, and in self-produced neighborhood productions. I knew intuitively, without a doubt, that I was worthy of fully allowing my creative spirit to have a loud and clear voice, and that it would be honored and received by the outer world as valuable, pleasing, and, in fact, quite wonderful! Putting my heart "out there" was the only way to go. It just never, ever occurred to me not to.

Then came the inner shutdown. I said "Bye-bye" to my confidence in opening my mouth and expressing my creative spirit, "Bye-bye" to my willingness to trust. And I said "Good-bye," too, to allowing my heart to lead and the Child in my heart to speak her truth.

Why do children shut down like this? It's due to something different for each of us, I imagine. Or, to put it more accurately, different combinations of unique life experiences and soul learnings cause each one of us to stop listening to the wisdom of the joyful Child in our heart, our God-essence. And, with rare exception, all of us do this to varying extent at some time during our soul's journey in "Schoolroom Earth."

In my case, it happened at about age twelve. The highlight (or lowlight, depending on your perspective) of my journey centers on my two junior high drama coaches, who each cast me in the cherished lead roles of the school play. Each also wore another hat: that of English teacher. It was under this authority that they chose to punish my sociable and loquacious classroom nature by taping my mouth shut and forcing me to sit outside the classroom door. Perfectly perched in the wide expanse of hall, I sat for any and all passersby to see. This was the "perfect" public humiliation and embarrassment for a creatively effervescent, yet sensitive young adolescent.

This was combined with my already present and fairly deep private sense of humiliation and embarrassment. My tendency to already feel "less than" was due mostly to living in the scary, sometimes volatile atmosphere that arises when a family member suffers from alcoholism. Given their preoccupation with other matters, including a thorny divorce, neither of my beloved parents chose to do a thing on my behalf about the horrific hallway situation, even when it occurred a second time.

And so, given the abusive teachers, the seemingly indifferent and preoccupied parents, and and the usual challenges of adolescent psycho-social maturation, I made a choice. Off I went to sleep—emotionally and spiritually, that is. The sleeping potion? The overwhelming hurt and sorrow engulfing "Little Suzanne."

I "woke up" about three decades later, following an "off with her head" ousting from the corporate healthcare world.

In essence, I suffered a creativity silencing eerily similar to the ones I'd experienced years before, though this differed in scope and method. These events, one might say, were metaphoric bookends on my life experience "bookshelf" during my 20s, 30s and 40s. These were years filled with extraordinary friendships, exciting travel, academic success, marriage, the birth of my amazing son, and a wonderful career. But these were also three decades of not fully following my heart, of cutting myself off from the expression of my creative life purpose, and of living a daily life very short on joy and very long on "yuck." In so many large and small ways, I dishonored my God-essence.

But this isn't a "woe was me" story. Quite the contrary! The Angels' Divine Love Letter is one of freedom, love, and new beginnings, of embracing our souls' journeys with joy and exuberance. The Angels tell us that it's never too late (or too early!) to remember that we have choices. We **always** have choices. We aren't victims of our life experiences unless we choose to be victims. We won't have daily lives devoid of joy unless we choose to live our lives devoid of joy. We aren't unworthy of receiving all that our hearts desire unless we choose to believe that we are unworthy.

We are **always** free to choose. And if we choose to honor the voice and wisdom of the joyful Child in our heart—our God-essence—our lives will unfold with great beauty, joy, harmony, and yes, ease. This will be true even when the soul's journey brings us (as it did in my case) a post wake-up spiritual path jam-packed with challenges such as separation, divorce, the death of five close loved ones, huge business and financial fluctuations, moves to new homes, disinheritence, a child's leaving home for college, and a plethora of other wonderful challenges!

Which brings me back to the story of my journey. My late 40s wake-up included not only guidance and direction by the Angels to heal the deep hurt around "Little Suzanne," but also a recruitment call to embrace my joyous, creative life's purpose in service to others as an intuitive healer and educator. As I've done this, I've experienced firsthand the abundant miracles that unfold when the joyful Child in my heart, my God-essence, leads the way. These miracles range from finding the best form for my business endeavors to assume, to finding opportunities to connect with wonderful potential life partners, to finding a beautiful, sacred living space when my current one was no longer an option!

And for me, for "Little Suzanne," my awakening goes back to the wonderful plush critters of my childhood. Little did I know then how profound the literal and metaphoric importance my beloved inanimate pets would be for me, how deeply they would inform my soul's journey here in "Schoolroom Earth." I didn't know how they would provide such an amazing, continual wellspring of pure, authentic, spiritual joy, as well as learning and healing. And I could never have predicted how they would, over time, provide the sacred connections to my evolving life's purpose as a healer and educator. Through them, I'm inspired to inspire others to heal their lives; to follow their hearts; to imagine and create a daily life of beauty, peace and joy; and to truly help create Heaven on Earth, *from the inside out!*

The Divine Love Letter

Today, This Very Moment

Dearest Reader,

Greetings! We invite you to let us tell
you of your Light, your unique and quite
astonishing Divine Light.

From our perspective, your Inner Brilliance
is truly breathtaking to behold.
Your heart shines like no other on this planet!

Please remember that, above all else,

you are a beautiful, beloved,

and perfect Child of God, of Divine Love!

Because this is who you *ARE*, you are worthy
of receiving all the miracles your heart
desires — in matters small and large, ordinary
and extraordinary — today, tomorrow,
and always!

Your life is a unique, important,
and sacred spiritual journey.
Infuse it with joy, curiosity and awe.

On your perfectly orchestrated life path, you will make no mistakes and you will experience no accidents.

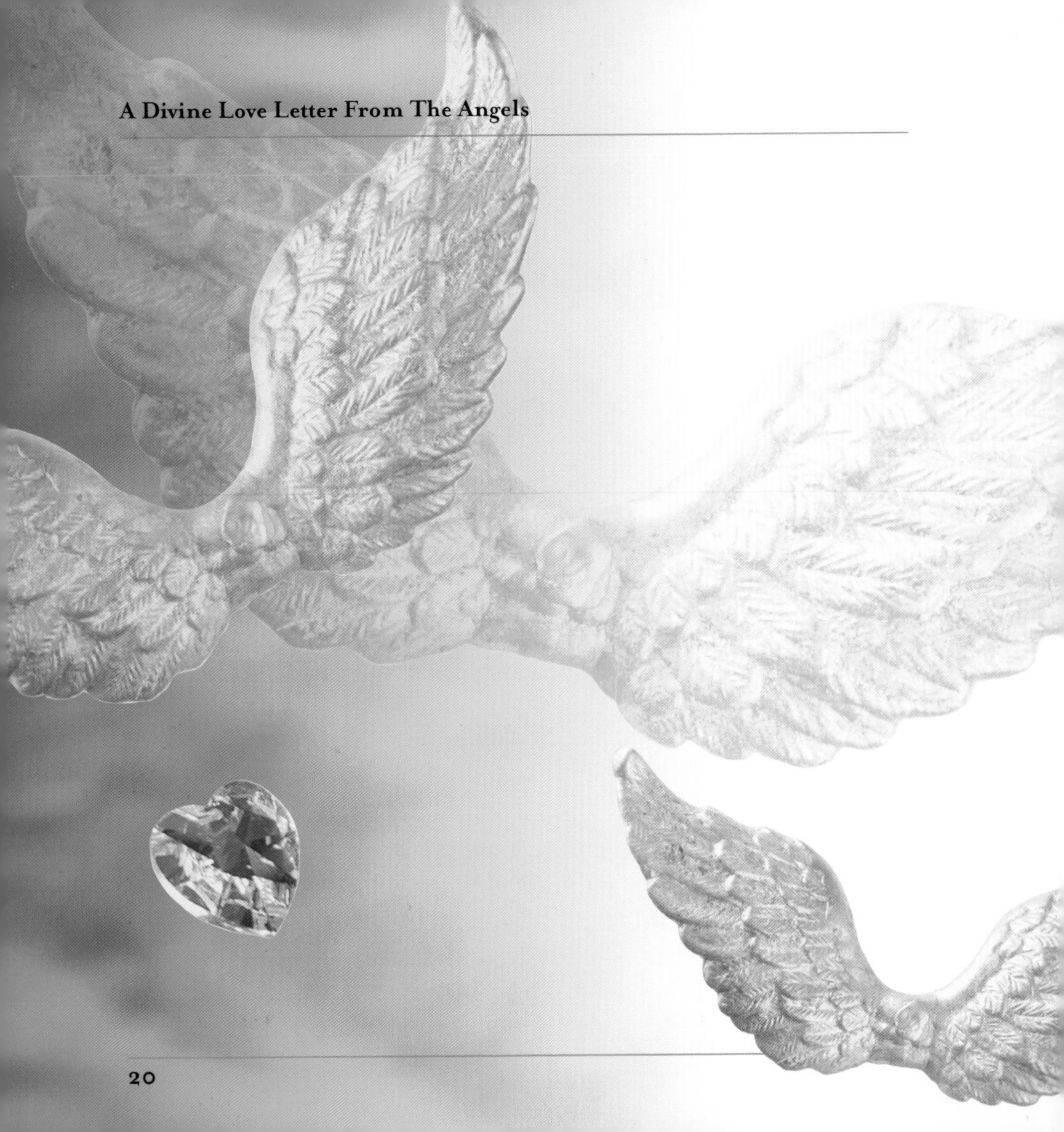

Instead, you will encounter only opportunities for Higher Learning. Embrace them with wonderment and gratitude.

Trust that you are always exactly where

you need to be in order to experience

your greatest good and expansion

as a beloved Child of God.

Your soul is here attending "Schoolroom Earth" to learn, grow, and fully remember your God-essence, and your sacred connection and Oneness with all of God's Creation!

Separation and separateness are illusions.

Please remember, too, that as you awaken to and embrace your Inner Light, you help create lasting peace, not only for you, but for all of Mother Earth's inhabitants.

It is true that only from peaceful souls

can humankind create a planet at peace!

*You are the co-creator of
your daily reality and your authentic
inner- and outer-world power.*

*As you take spiritual responsibility
for your life, you surrender the
illusion of control and create space
for Divine Order and Divine Timing.*

A Divine Love Letter From The Angels

When you take spiritual responsibility
for your life, abundant miracles unfold
for you and all of your loved ones.

*You are also free in every moment
to choose to live with joy and presence,
guided by your heart.*

*Know that you are always — in all ways —
fully supported by Divine Love.
And only Divine Love is real.
Fear is an illusion.*

Please remember that it is a sacred endeavor to honor, cherish, and put yourself— your amazing God-essence— first in your day-to-day life.

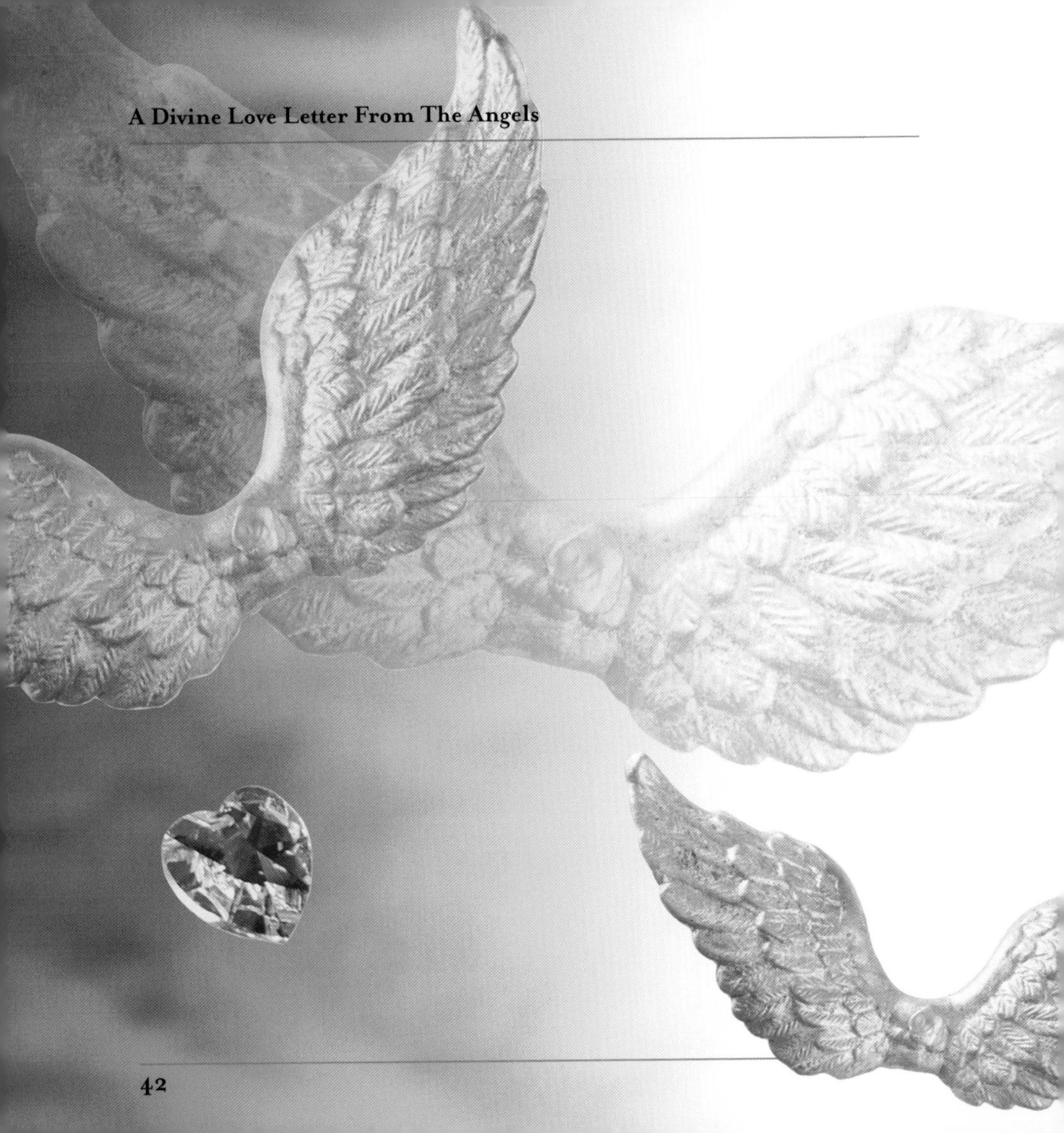

Only when you are full and whole in body, mind, heart, and spirit can you effectively give to and help others.

A Divine Love Letter From The Angels

Take time often to breathe, to be still,

and to listen to your God-essence within.

Release the past, let go of the future, embrace the present moment.

Be kind, gentle, compassionate,
and patient with yourself.
And remember to forgive yourself,
over and over and over and over.

Honor your emotions. Allow them
to connect you with others, with your own
God-essence, and with Divine Love.

Remember that all emotions and feelings are sacred. Along with your intuition, they will always yield your Higher Truth.

The Child in your heart, Little You,
holds the key to unlimited intuitive wisdom
and transformative healing guidance.

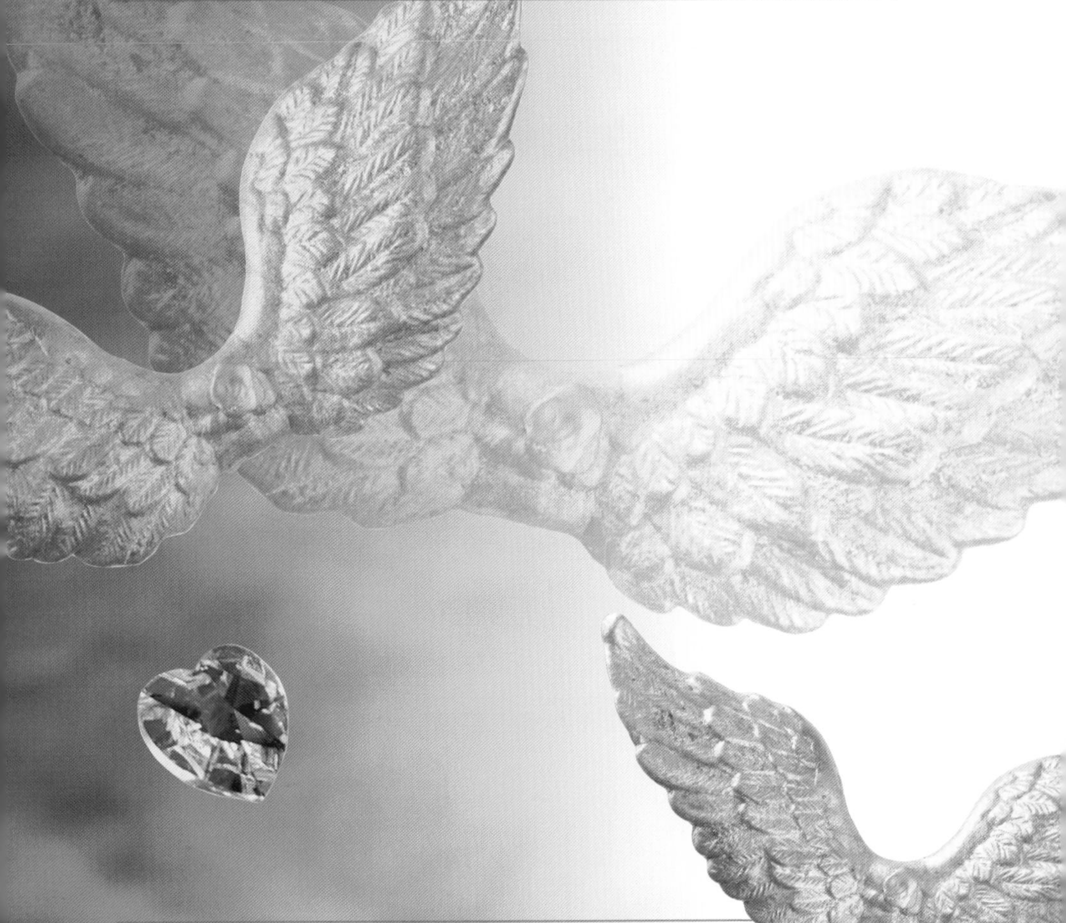

He or she knows all that you need—

in truth, all that your heart desires —

to create a life of joy, harmony, abundance,

and creative expression.

*Honor, celebrate, and play
with this beautiful, amazing,
and innocent Child within.*

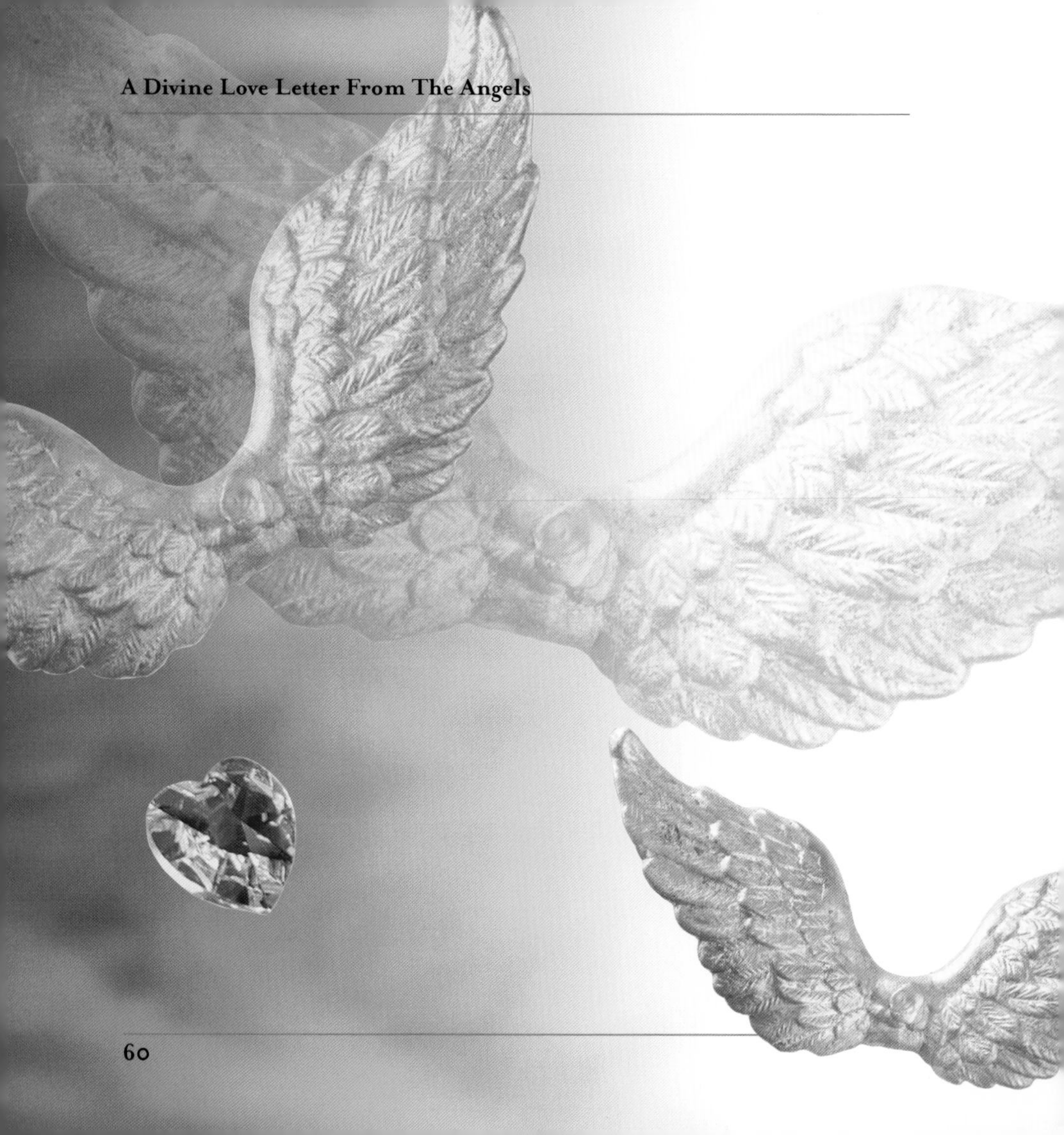

Trust him or her to lead you to all the treasures of Divine Love and Light awaiting you inside. They are spectacular and endless!

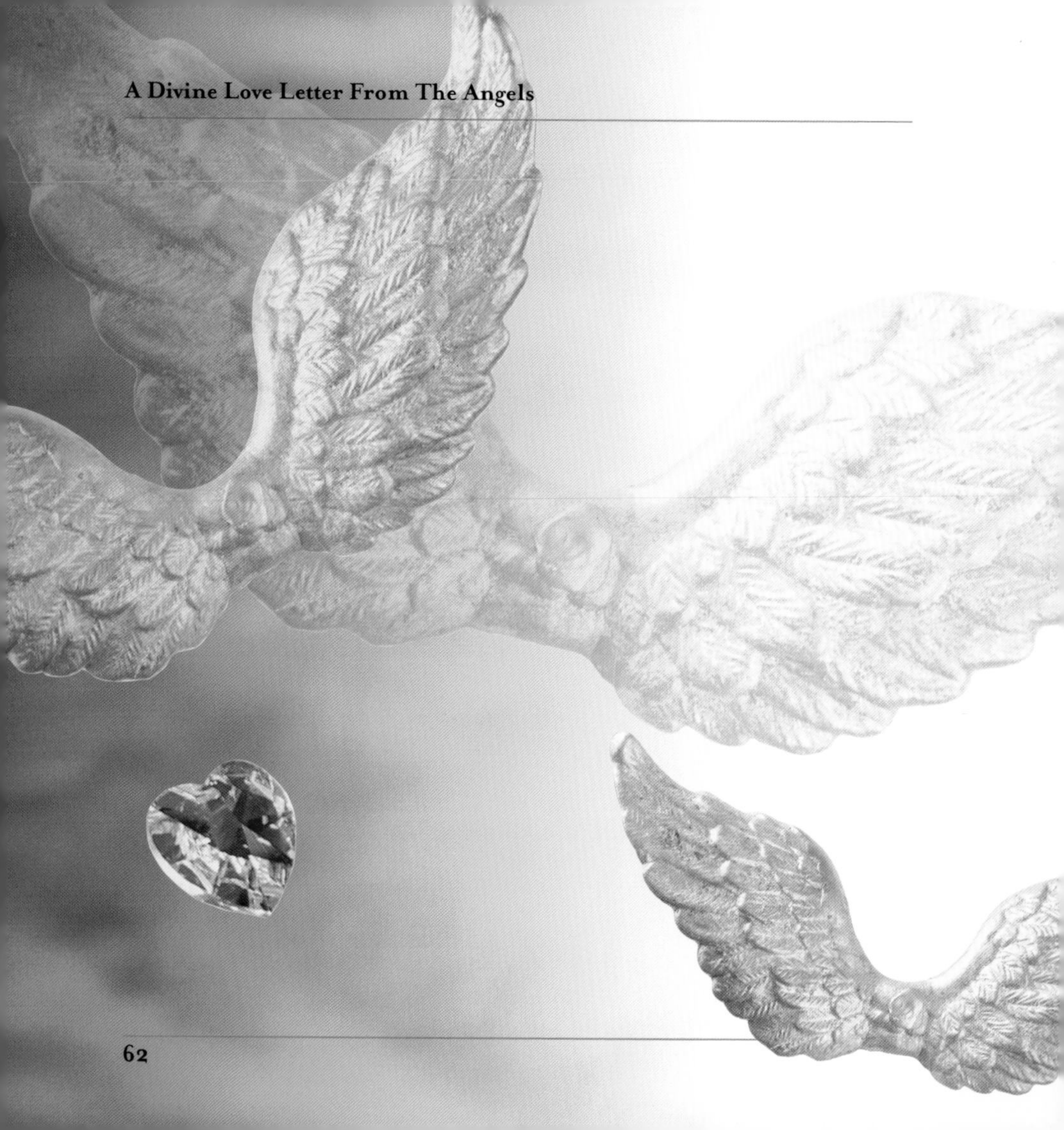

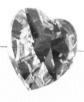

We are always present, willing to assist and guide you. Invite us in!

We answer in action— with signs, symbols, metaphors, miracles, and "ah-ha's"!

A Divine Love Letter From The Angels

Blessings of magnificent and joyful new beginnings — from the inside out!

All Our Love,

The Angels

p.s. Everything changes when you do!

Using this Book to Welcome Angelic Guidance

It is a very easy matter to begin receiving the wonderful and highly useful guidance available to you from the Angels. Because you're reading this, you've already begun! The Angels' Love Letter presented to you in this book is the ideal starting point, because it can provide the perfect inspiration and guidance for you, wherever you are on your life journey and wherever you are on your personal spiritual path. The words, phrases, and the feelings they'll evoke—in fact, the entire experience of reading this book—will speak to you with poignancy and truth as you open yourself to the experience of receiving the amazing messages and astonishing pure Divine Love contained within it.

The Love Letter is intended to be read initially as you would any long-awaited correspondence from a special loved one, straight through, beginning to end, in one sitting. Perhaps another time you'd like some general guidance for your day. Maybe you need advice about a particular issue or situation you're dealing with in your life. Along my spiritual journey, I have especially enjoyed simply asking the Angels for assistance and then receiving the guidance by opening one of my favorite spiritual guidance books to a random page. There, I always find what I'm seeking: understanding that is pertinent to the topic at hand! If this method resonates with you, I suggest that you try it with this book, focusing on the Divine Love Letter section. Whatever insight you need will be there, awaiting your reflection. Enjoy!

About the Author

Suzanne Bennett is an inspirational Angel intuitive, educator, author, and co-creative healer specializing in joyfully awakening, celebrating, and healing the Divine Child in your heart. She holds a bachelor of arts degree in humanities and a master's degree in public health. A former health administrator, researcher, innovator, writer, and developer, she has devoted the past five years to refining her angelically-guided intuition and to educating the planet about the transformative healing power of Divine Love.

In 2000 Suzanne co-founded HeartSense, A Spa for the Spirit! in St. Paul, Minnesota. Her current endeavors

present new facets of Suzanne's unique heart-opening spark of spiritual joy, laughter, miracle consciousness, and clairsentient insight. Her angelically-guided training encompasses the wisdom of the twelve Archangels, Masters, Guides, and Suzanne's soul knowledge and life journey experience. She is not aligned with any particular religion or tradition.

Suzanne lives in St. Paul, Minnesota with her son, her cat Batcat, and a myriad of plush companions. Her ongoing personal healing practice embraces universal spiritual themes, reflections, and wisdom. Suzanne is committed to helping create lasting peace for Mother Earth and each of Her inhabitants, *from the inside out!*